The Wisdom of Meister Eckhart

THE
WISDOM
OF
MEISTER
ECKHART

Compiled and introduced by
Oliver Davies

This edition copyright © 1999 Lion Publishing

Published by
Lion Publishing plc
Sandy Lane West, Oxford, England
www.lion-publishing.co.uk
ISBN 0 7459 4217 2

First edition 1999
10 9 8 7 6 5 4 3 2 1 0

All rights reserved

A catalogue record for this book is available
from the British Library

Typeset in 12.5/13 Venetian 301
Printed and bound in Singapore

CONTENTS

INTRODUCTION

Eckhart is one of the greatest of medieval mystics. He was born in 1260 in Hocheim in eastern Germany, and was educated as a Dominican at the nearby priory in Erfurt. He may have gone from there to Paris, which was the leading centre of learning in the medieval world; our earliest record of him shows that he was certainly studying and teaching in Paris by 1294. He was rapidly promoted to offices of administrative responsibility and pastoral care in the Dominican Order, and spent much of his life travelling widely throughout Europe in fulfilment of his duties. He returned to Paris on two occasions, to teach as one of the foremost theologians of his day. Towards the end of his life, however, Meister Eckhart fell victim to political intrigue and, despite the strong support of his Order, some aspects of his teaching were condemned by Papal decree in 1329, probably shortly after his death. Modern scholarship has exonerated Meister Eckhart from the suspicions of his own day, and he is now held in high honour.

Throughout Eckhart's work there is a persistent sense of the power of God and of our own emptiness and receptivity before him. In many diverse and often highly imaginative ways, Eckhart explored the dynamic relation between our own interior self and the fertile presence of the triune God. The emphasis in his sermons, therefore, is not upon sanctifying works and action in the world, but rather upon that transformation in the spirit which sanctifies us and thus makes all our works good. Time and again, Eckhart draws the attention of his listeners back to what is most essential, to the God-given potentiality for knowing God and becoming one with him that lies in the depths of our being. The many different approaches to this 'spark of the soul' which he develops serve to remind us that it is a potentiality which escapes our own reasoning and imagining; it is to be thought of as 'neither this nor that', 'more unknown than known'. And yet, as the place where God gives birth to himself in us, it is the transformative centre of our life.

Meister Eckhart's message is a timeless one of hope. His view of the dynamic power of God, intimately known to us in the innermost part of our being, is an inspiring vision both of the nature of God and of what it means to be human. His mystical understanding of the liberating and transforming action of the self-birthing God at the centre of our being transcends his own age and remains as vital and alive to us today as it was for those who first heard him speak in fourteenth-century Germany.

OLIVER DAVIES

GOD IN
HIMSELF

I

GOD'S INFINITY

God is infinite in his simplicity and simple in his infinity. Therefore he is everywhere and is everywhere complete. He is everywhere on account of his infinity, and is everywhere complete on account of his simplicity. Only God flows into all things, their very essences. Nothing else flows into something else. God is in the innermost part of each and every thing, only in its innermost part, and he alone is *one*.

GOD'S TRANSCENDENCE

There is something which is above the created being of the soul and which is untouched by any createdness, by any nothingness. Even the angels do not have this, whose clear being is pure and deep; even that does not touch it. It is like the divine nature; in itself it is one and has nothing in common with anything. And it is with regard to this that many teachers go wrong. It is a strange land, a wilderness, being more nameless than with name, more unknown than known.

GOD'S POWER

I have said often enough that there is a power in the soul which is untouched by either time or flesh. It flows from the spirit and remains within the spirit and is entirely spiritual by nature. Now God is green and flowering in this power in all the joy and all the honour which he is in himself. There is such great delight there and such inconceivably deep joy that no one can adequately describe it... If someone possessed an entire kingdom or all the goods of the earth, and if they gave it all up for the sake of God, becoming one of the poorest of the earth, and if God then gave that person as much suffering as he has ever given anyone, and if they had to endure this all their life long, and if God then allowed them to glimpse just once and for only a fraction of a second how he is in this power, their joy would be so great that all of this suffering and all of this poverty would be insignificant.

4
GOD'S WORD

The Father speaks the Son with the whole of his
power and speaks all things in him. All creatures
are the utterance of God. If my mouth speaks
and declares God, so too does the being of a
stone, and we understand more by works than
by words.

GOD'S GOODNESS

Now take note of what we must have if we are
to dwell in him, that is in God. There are three
things we must have. The first is that we should
take leave of ourselves and of all things and be
attached to nothing external which acts upon
the senses within, and also that we should not
remain in any creature which is either in time
or in eternity. The second is that we should
not love this or that good thing but rather
goodness as such from which all good things
flow, for things are only desirable and delightful
in so far as God is in them. Therefore we should
not love any good thing more than the extent
to which we love God in it, nor should we love
God for the sake of his heavenly kingdom nor
for the sake of anything else, but we should
love him for his goodness which he is in himself.
For whoever loves him for anything else does
not dwell in him but dwells in that for the sake
of which they love him. Therefore, if you wish

to dwell in him, you must love him for his sake alone. The third is that we should not take God as he is good or just, but we should take him in the pure and clear substance in which he possesses himself. For goodness and justice are a garment of God, since they enfold him. Strip away from God, therefore, everything which clothes him and take him in his dressing room where he is naked and bare in himself. Thus you will remain in him.

6

GOD'S LOVE

There is a great difference between God's love and our love. We only love something in so far as we find God in it. Even if I had sworn to do otherwise, I could love nothing but goodness. But God loves to the extent that he is good… and loves us in so far as we are in him and in his love. This is his gift: it is the gift of his love that we are in him and dwell 'in wisdom'.

DETACHMENT

DIVINE KNOWLEDGE

Neither the skills of all creatures, nor your own wisdom, nor the whole extent of your knowledge can bring you to the point where you have a divine knowledge of God. If you wish to know God in a divine manner, then your knowing must become a pure unknowing, a forgetting of yourself and of all creatures.

THE SPARK OF THE SOUL

Therefore I say that when we turn away from ourselves and from all created things, to that extent we are united and sanctified in the soul's spark, which is untouched by either space or time. This spark is opposed to all creatures and desires nothing but God, naked, just as he is in himself.

FREEDOM AND SIMPLICITY

We must learn to free ourselves of ourselves in all our gifts, not holding on to what is our own, or seeking anything, either profit, pleasure, inwardness, sweetness, reward, heaven or our own will… Where God finds his own will, he gives himself and enters in with all that he is. And the more we cease to be in our own will, the more truly we begin to be in God's will. Thus it is not enough for us to give ourselves up just once, together with all that we have and are capable of, but we must renew ourselves constantly, thus preserving our freedom and simplicity in all things.

TRUE PENANCE

Many people think that they should do great works in external things, such as fasting, walking barefoot and such like; things which we call penances. But the truest and best penance with which we make the greatest improvement is when we turn inwardly from all things which are not God and are not divine, and turn wholly towards God with an unshakeable love so that our devotion and our desire for him become great.

TAKING LEAVE OF OURSELVES

You must give yourself up, and must do so completely, if you are really to renounce something. Once a man came to me – this happened quite recently – and told me that he had given away great amounts of land and possessions in order to save his soul. But I thought to myself: what small and insignificant things you have given away. To contemplate what you have renounced is blindness and stupidity. But if you have abandoned yourself, then you have really renounced something. Those who have taken leave of themselves are so pure that the world cannot endure them.

MAKING SPACE FOR GOD

As far as you depart from all things, thus far,
no less and no more, does God enter into you,
with all that is his.

POSSESSION

DESIRING GOD

Whoever possesses God in their being, has him in a divine manner, and he shines out to them in all things; for them all things taste of God and in all things it is God's image that they see. God is always radiant in them; they are inwardly detached from the world and are informed by the loving presence of their God. It is the same as when someone has a great thirst and, although they may be doing something other than drinking and their minds may be turned to other things, the thought of a drink will not leave them for as long as they thirst, whatever they do, whoever they are with, whatever they strive for, whatever their works or thoughts; and the greater their thirst, the greater, the more intense, immediate and persistent the thought of a drink becomes. Or if someone loves something passionately with all their might, so that nothing else pleases them or touches their heart, and they desire that alone and nothing else, then certainly whoever it may be, or whoever they may be with, whatever they are doing or are setting out to do, the object of their love will never be extinguished in them, but they will find its image in all things, and the greater their love becomes, the more present to them it will be. Such a person does not seek peace, for it is already theirs.

KNOWING GOD

I have spoken of a power in the soul. In its first outreach it does not grasp God in so far as he is good, nor does it grasp God in so far as he is truth. It penetrates further, to the ground of God, and then further still, until it grasps God in his unity and in his desert. It grasps God in his wilderness and his own ground. Therefore it does not rest content with anything, but seeks further for what God is in his divinity and in his own nature.

RECEIVING GOD

God wants to be entirely our possession. This is what he wills and seeks, and that is why he is as he is. This is the cause of his greatest bliss and joy. And the more he can be our possession, the greater is his bliss and joy, for the more we are in possession of other things, the less we possess him, and the less love we have for other things, the more we receive him with all that he offers us.

POSSESSING GOD

In return for keeping us detached from things
which are outside us, God wishes to give us
for our own possession all that is in heaven,
even heaven itself together with all its powers,
indeed with everything which ever flowed from
it and which angels and saints enjoy, so that all
this may be ours too, far more than any *thing*
has ever been ours. In return for stripping my
self of myself for his sake, God will be wholly
my own possession with all that he is and can
do, as much mine as his, no more and no less.

ENJOYING GOD

There are people who enjoy God in one way but not in another. They only want to possess God in one way of devotion and not in another. I will say no more about this, but it is nevertheless quite wrong. Whoever wants to receive God properly must receive him equally in all things, in oppression as in prosperity, in tears as in joy. Always and everywhere he is the same.

GOD IN US

GOD FILLS OUR EMPTINESS

Now know this! God can leave nothing empty; neither God nor nature can tolerate emptiness in anything. Therefore, if it seems to you at present that you cannot feel his presence and that you are entirely empty of him, then this is not in fact the case. For if there is something empty beneath heaven, whatever it may be – large or small – heaven will draw it up to itself, or heaven will have to descend to it and fill it with itself. God, who is the master of nature, cannot tolerate emptiness in anything. Therefore remain still and do not waver from this emptiness, for if you turn away from it at this point you shall never be able to find it again.

FILLED WITH GOD

To be empty of all creatures is to be filled with God, and to be filled with all creatures is to be empty of God.

THE SON IS BORN IN US

The Father has only one Son, and the less we turn our intention and attention to things other than God and the more we turn to nothing external, all the more shall we be transformed in the Son and all the more shall the Son be born in us and we be born in the Son and become one Son. Our Lord Jesus Christ is the sole Son of the Father, and he alone is both human and divine. But there is only a single Son in a single being, which is divine being. Thus we become one in him when he is the one object of our attention.

LIVING WITHOUT A WHY

This is how the Son is born in us – when we live without a Why and are born again into the Son.

GOD ACTS IN THE EMPTY SOUL

'Rise up!' (Luke 8:54). Our Lord placed his hand on the girl and said: 'Rise up!' The 'hand of God' is the Holy Spirit. All works are performed by warmth, for if the fiery love of God grows cold in the soul, the soul will die, and if God is to act in the soul, then God must be united with her. If the soul is to be united with God, she must be separated from all things and must be as solitary as God is solitary. A work which God performs in an empty soul is more precious than heaven and earth. It is for this that God created the soul, that she should be united with him.

GOD IN OUR HEART

The real possession of God is to be found
in the heart, in an inner motion of the spirit
towards him and striving for him, and not just
in thinking about him always and in the same
way. For that would be beyond the capacity
of our nature and would be very difficult to
achieve and would not even be the best thing
to do. We should not content ourselves with a
God of thoughts for, when the thoughts come
to an end, so too shall God. Rather, we should
have a living God who is beyond the thoughts
of all people and all creatures. That kind of God
will not leave us, unless we ourselves choose
to turn away from him.

GOD IS LOVE

The love that someone gives contains not two
but one and oneness, and when I love I am more
God than I am in myself.

GOD'S GIFTS

LOVE

Penances are done in order to constrain the flesh, but if you lay upon it the bridle of love, then you will tame and control it in a way that is a thousand times better... Therefore God intends nothing for us so much as love. For love is just the same as the fisherman's hook: the fisherman cannot lay hold of the fish unless it is attached to the hook. If it has swallowed the hook, the fisherman can be sure of his fish, whichever way it turns, this way or that, he knows he will get it. I say the same of love: they who are caught by it have the strongest bonds and the sweetest burden... They can endure cheerfully all that befalls them and that God sends them, and they can cheerfully forgive all the evil that others do to them. Nothing brings you closer to God and gives you God so much as this sweet bond of love. Whoever has found this path does not leave it again.

I have upon occasion explained what a just
person is, but now I give it another meaning:
a just person is someone who is established
in justice and who is transformed into justice.
The just man or woman lives in God and God
lives in them, for God is born in the just as
they are in him, since every one of the just
person's virtues gives birth to God and brings
him joy. And not only every virtue of the just,
but also every good work, however small it may
be, which is done through the just person and
in justice, gives God joy, filling him with joy,
for nothing remains in its ground which is not
thrilled through and through with joy. Those
who are slow of understanding should simply
accept this, while those who are enlightened
should know it.

PEACE

As far as you are in God, thus far you are in peace, and as far as you are outside God, thus far you are outside peace. If only something is in God, then it has peace. It is in peace in so far as it is in God. And you can tell how far you are in God or not by the extent to which you have peace or not. For where you lack peace, you must necessarily lack peace, since lack of peace comes from the creature and not from God.

PATIENCE

If you have failings, then ask God frequently
in prayer if it may not be to his honour and
pleasure to take them from you, for you can do
nothing without his help. If he does so, then
thank him, and if he does not, then bear them
for his sake, though not as the failings of sin
but as a great exercise in which you can earn
a reward and practise patience. You should be
content whether he grants you the gift or not.

HUMILITY

Those who have destroyed themselves as they exist in themselves, in God and in all creatures, have taken up the lowest position, and God must pour the whole of himself into them — or he would not be God. I declare the good, eternal and everlasting truth that God must pour himself according to the whole of his capacity into all those who have abandoned themselves to the very ground of their being, and he must do so so completely that he can hold nothing back of all his life, all his being and nature, even of his divinity, which he must pour fully and in a fructifying way into those who have abandoned themselves for God and have taken up the lowest position.

THE GIFT OF GOD

We must train ourselves not to seek or strive for our own interests in anything, but rather to find and to grasp God in all things. For God does not give us anything in order that we should enjoy its possession and rest content with it, nor has he ever done so. All the gifts which he has ever granted us in heaven or on earth were given solely in order to be able to give us the *one* gift, which is himself.

Text acknowledgments

Extracts 1–9, 11, 13, 16, 18 and 20–30 taken from *Meister Eckhart: Selected Writings*,
selected and translated Oliver Davies, Penguin Books Ltd, 1994

Extracts 10, 12, 14–15, 17 and 19 taken from *The Rhineland Mystics: An Anthology*,
edited Oliver Davies, SPCK, 1989

Picture acknowledgments

1, 13, 23: The Table of the Seven Deadly Sins (detail) by Hieronymus Bosch
(c. 1450–1516), Prado, Madrid, Spain/Bridgeman Art Library, London/New York; 2, 37:
The Maelbeke Altarpiece (detail) attributed to Jan van Eyck/Christie's Images; 9: The
Landauer Altarpiece, All Saints' Day, 1511 (detail) by Albrecht Dürer (1471–1528),
Kunsthistorisches Museum, Vienna, Austria/Bridgeman Art Library, London/New York;
17, cover: An Angel with a Soul at the edge of Hell (detail) by a follower of Hieronymus
Bosch/Christie's Images; 25, 35: Left panel from the Ghent Altarpiece, 1432 (detail) by
Jan van Eyck (c. 1390–1441), St Bavo Cathedral, Ghent, Belgium/Giraudon/Bridgeman
Art Library, London/New York; 33: Adoration of the Magi: Whole Triptych (detail) by
Hans Memling (c. 1433–94), Prado, Madrid, Spain/Bridgeman Art Library, London/New
York; 41: Christ as the Redeemer by a follower of Quinten Massys/Christie's Images.

All artwork by Vanessa Card